KS2 SATs Practice Papers

4 English Grammar, Punctuation & Spelling Tests for Year 6

Volume I

New Edition for 2019-2020

With FREE ADDITIONAL CONTENT Online

Ages 10-11

About this Book & How to Use It

This book is for Year 6 students and contains **4 complete, fully up-to-date** Grammar, Punctuation & Spelling Practice Tests, each of which is **closely modelled** on one of the **most recent** SATs Paper 1 exams — **including the 2019 exam**.

Like the actual exam, each Practice Test should be completed in **45 minutes** and consists of **46 to 50 questions** that assess the student's knowledge of English **grammar**, **punctuation** and **spelling**.

Also included for students are
◊ Practice **Cover Sheets**.
◊ Easy-to-understand **Instructions** providing information about the types of questions they will meet; the kinds of answers required; mark schemes; and time.

At the end of the book, parents and teachers will find
◊ The **complete Answers** for all four tests plus their **full Marking Guidelines**.

We recommend that
◊ Students attempt these tests in a **quiet environment**.
◊ Students work through these tests in order (as their **difficulty level increases** each time).
◊ These tests are used to **identify the areas** where students excel and those which they find challenging.
◊ The marks obtained by students in these tests are used as an **indication** of their progress.

Good luck!

Get your
FREE
ADDITIONAL CONTENT ONLINE
with this QR code:

Includes a printable HOW WELL I DID pamphlet
PLUS a list of KEY SPaG TERMS & PHRASES for PAPER 1

Want even more? Then why not explore
our growing collection of
FREE PRINTABLE
EDUTAINMENT & EDUCATIONAL RESOURCES?
Find them here:

Includes printable worksheets, word lists
& word games!

Alternatively, you can get your
Free Additional Content Online for this book @ **http://bit.ly/2um7JRV**
Free Edutainment & Educational Resources @ **www.swottotspublishing.com/free-from-stp-books**

Published by STP Books
An imprint of Swot Tots Publishing Ltd
Kemp House
152-160 City Road
London EC1V 2NX

www.swottotspublishing.com

Text, design, and layout © Swot Tots Publishing Ltd

First published 2018 by Swot Tots Publishing Ltd
This edition published January 2020 by STP Books

STP Books have asserted their moral right under the Copyright, Designs and Patents Act, 1988, to be identified as the author of this work.

All rights reserved. Without limiting the rights under copyright reserved above, no part of this publication may be reproduced, stored in a retrieval system, or transmitted in any form or by any means electronic, mechanical, photocopying, printing, recording, or otherwise without either the prior permission of the publishers or a licence permitting restricted copying in the United Kingdom issued by the Copyright Licensing Agency Limited, 5th Floor, Shackleton House, Hay's Galleria, 4 Battle Bridge Lane, London SE1 2HX.

Typeset, cover design, and inside concept design by Swot Tots Publishing Ltd.

British Library Cataloguing-in-Publication Data. A catalogue record for this book is available from the British Library.

ISBN 978-1-912956-08-1

CONTENTS

Instructions for Students 4

ENGLISH GRAMMAR, PUNCTUATION & SPELLING PRACTICE TEST PAPERS

Practice Test Paper 1 *5*
Practice Test Paper 2 *19*
Practice Test Paper 3 *33*
Practice Test Paper 4 *47*

ANSWERS & MARKING GUIDELINES

Notes to Using the Answers & Marking Guidelines *61*

Practice Test Paper 1: Answers & Marking Guidelines *62*
Practice Test Paper 2: Answers & Marking Guidelines *64*
Practice Test Paper 3: Answers & Marking Guidelines *66*
Practice Test Paper 4: Answers & Marking Guidelines *68*

INSTRUCTIONS FOR STUDENTS

PLEASE READ THE FOLLOWING INSTRUCTIONS <u>CAREFULLY</u> BEFORE PROCEEDING WITH ANY OF THE PRACTICE TEST PAPERS IN THIS BOOK.

Questions & Answers

In each Practice Test Paper in this book, your grammar, punctuation and spelling are assessed. Each Paper contains different types of questions for you to answer in different ways.

Each question heading will make it clear to you what type of answer is needed, including the following:

- Multiple-Choice Answers
- Short Written Answers
- Ticking Boxes
- Circling or Underlining Words
- Connecting Boxes
- Filling in Boxes

Marks

Beside each question, on the right-hand side of the page, you will find a number followed by the words 'mark' or 'marks'. This tells you the maximum number of marks each answer is worth.

Time

You have 45 minutes to complete each Paper. Work through each Paper as quickly, but as carefully, as you can. If you finish before the 45 minutes are up, go back and check your work.

Good luck!

ENGLISH GRAMMAR, PUNCTUATION & SPELLING

PRACTICE TEST 1

KS2 SATs Year 6   English   Paper 1: Questions

First name: _____

Middle name: _____

Last name: _____

Date of birth: _____

School name: _____

Total score: _____ / 50

1 Show which sentence must end with a **question mark**.

Tick one.

I asked how she had done that ☐

How did you do that ☐

Show me how to do that ☐

I want to know how you did that ☐

1 mark

2 Draw a line to connect each word to the correct **suffix**. You may use each suffix only once.

Word   **Suffix**

power   able

child   ment

comfort   less

amuse   hood

1 mark

3 Show whether each sentence is a **question** or a **command**. Tick one box in each row.

SENTENCE	Question	Command
Don't scare the birds		
Don't forget to feed the cat		
Don't you ever groom your pony		
Don't go near that dog		

1 mark

4 Insert one **comma** in the correct place in the following sentence.

Katy was late for school again so she began to run.

1 mark

5 Draw a line to connect each **prefix** to the correct word. You may use each prefix only once.

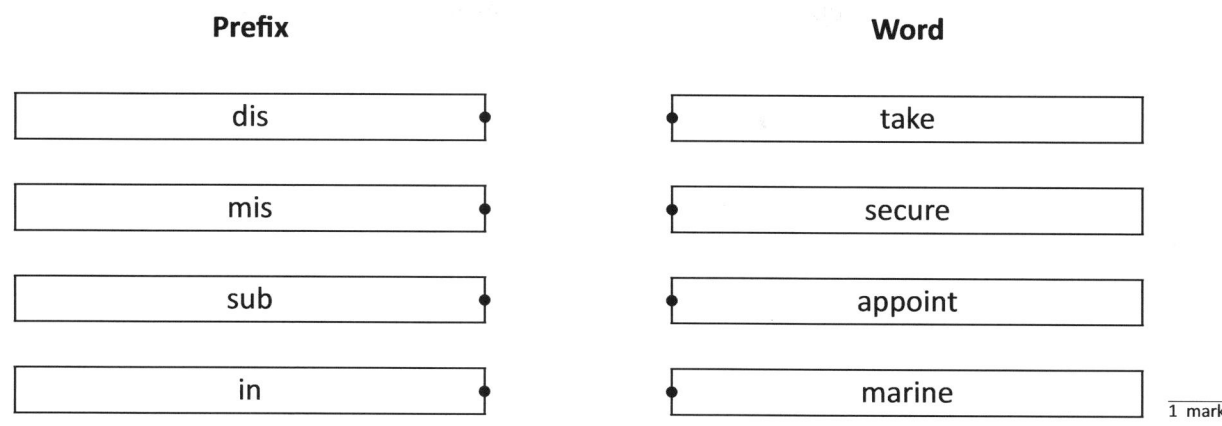

1 mark

6 Show which sentence must **not** end with an **exclamation mark**.

Tick one.

What terrible weather we are having ☐

How cold it is today ☐

What an awful storm that was ☐

Make sure you take an umbrella ☐

1 mark

7 In each of the following, circle the word that completes the sentence so that it uses **Standard English**.

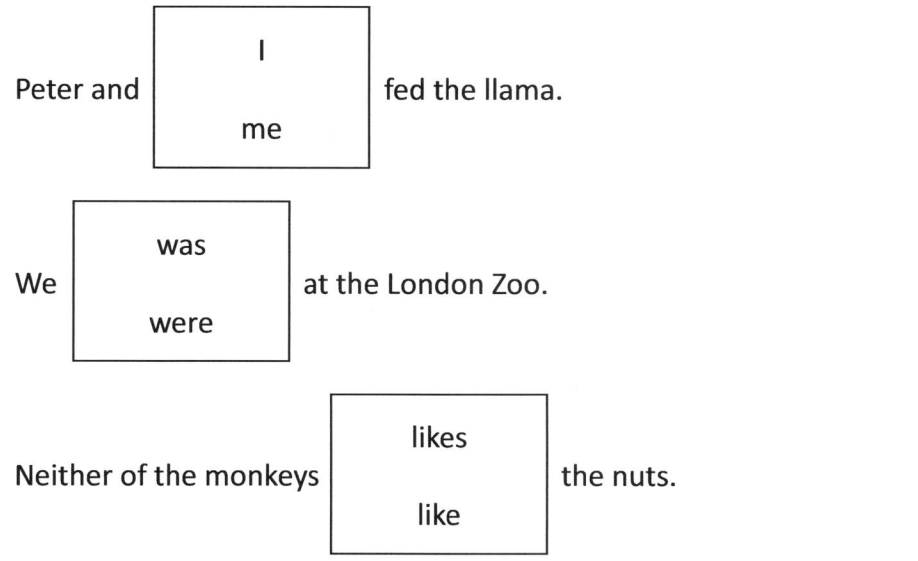

1 mark

Practice Test Paper 1   7

8 Complete the following sentence by inserting a **relative pronoun**.

The film _____ I watched yesterday was exceedingly boring.

1 mark

9 Show which sentence uses the word present as a **verb**.

Tick one.

The mayor was present at the meeting today. ☐

The mayor is busy at present. ☐

The mayor gave his son a present. ☐

The mayor is going to present the prizes. ☐

1 mark

10 Insert a **semi-colon** in the correct place in the following sentence.

Jane wanted to play tennis her brother preferred to have a game of squash.

1 mark

11 Insert a **pair of brackets** in the correct place in the following sentence.

The orang-utan one of the great apes is an endangered species.

1 mark

12 Show the meaning of the **prefix** inter in the words interfere, international and internet.

Tick one.

across ☐

between ☐

against ☐

distant ☐

1 mark

8 *Practice Test Paper 1*

13 Show which sentence has been punctuated correctly.

Tick one.

Some tourists probably from Germany — asked me the way to the station. ☐

Some tourists — probably from Germany — asked me the way to the station. ☐

Some tourists — probably from Germany asked me — the way to the station. ☐

Some tourists probably — from Germany asked me the way to the station. ☐

1 mark

14 Identify the word that is a **synonym** of deserted.

All the rats deserted the sinking ship.

Tick one.

boarded ☐

sailed ☐

abandoned ☐

crowded ☐

1 mark

15 Show which sentence is the most **formal**.

Tick one.

Would you care for another cup of tea? ☐

That was a lovely cup of tea, wasn't it? ☐

If I was you, I'd have a cup of tea. ☐

If you had asked, I would've made you a cuppa. ☐

1 mark

16 Show where a **hyphen** is needed in the following sentence. Tick one box.

Bernie had some carrot sticks, cherry tomatoes, a banana and a sugar free drink for lunch.

1 mark

Practice Test Paper 1   9

17 Identify the **word class** of <u>since</u> in the following sentence.

Martha has been absent from school <u>since</u> Wednesday.

	Tick one.
a pronoun	☐
a conjunction	☐
a preposition	☐
an adjective	☐

1 mark

18 Circle the two words that are **synonyms** in the following passage.

There are many enthralling stories of the courageous deeds of King Arthur's knights. Perhaps the most valiant and chivalrous one of all was Sir Gawain.

1 mark

19 Name the kind of **clause** that is underlined in the following sentence.

As his sister was busy feeding the cat, <u>Suresh hid her phone under the sofa</u>.

_____

1 mark

20 Insert a **dash** in the correct place in the following sentence.

Nobody could find Jason he was hiding in the garden.

1 mark

21 Identify the **word class** of the underlined word.

Do you want pizza, <u>or</u> do your prefer lasagne?

Tick one.

a co-ordinating conjunction ☐

a subordinating conjunction ☐

a possessive pronoun ☐

a relative pronoun ☐

1 mark

22 Insert a **colon** in the correct place in the following sentence.

Aunt May refuses to go camping she is afraid of being bitten or stung by insects or creepy crawlies.

1 mark

23 Insert three **commas** in the correct places in the following sentence.

Gerald enjoys swimming playing basketball rock climbing reading detective novels and making models.

1 mark

24 Show which sentence uses **tense** correctly.

Tick one.

When Patrick says he has finished his homework, his mother looked surprised. ☐

When Patrick said he had finished his homework, his mother looks surprised. ☐

When Patrick had said he had finished his homework, his mother looks surprised. ☐

When Patrick said he had finished his homework, his mother looked surprised. ☐

1 mark

25 Draw a line under the sentence that is the most **formal** in the following passage.

Don't forget we're going on holiday next week! We're gonna have a whale of a time! Wish you could make it. I will call you on our return.

1 mark

26 Circle the word that shows that the following sentence is a **command**.

Please remain seated until the seatbelt sign is off.

1 mark

27 Use **(S) subject** or **(O) object** to label each box.

We haven't any cake left as Giles ate it all last night.

1 mark

28 Rewrite each of the underlined verbs in the **simple past**.

When Susie goes to the pool, she always swims ten lengths.

1 mark

29 Show which sentence is closest in meaning to the one below.

Danny can't go skiing because he has broken his leg.

Tick one.

Danny's leg is broken now. ☐

Danny broke his leg while skiing. ☐

Danny broke his leg last week. ☐

Danny is in hospital with a broken leg. ☐

1 mark

12 Practice Test Paper 1

30 Circle the three **adjectives** in the following sentence.

Looking exhausted as he climbed the steep stairs, the lawyer seemed really unwell.

1 mark

31 Show which sentence is punctuated correctly.

Tick one.

Harry asked hopefully, "is there anything for supper?" ☐

Harry asked hopefully, "Is there anything for supper?" ☐

Harry asked hopefully, is there anything for supper." ☐

Harry asked hopefully "Is there anything for supper?" ☐

1 mark

32 Show which underlined word is an **adverb**.

Tick one.

The giant was huge and <u>ugly</u>. ☐

The monster glared with <u>hard</u>, angry eyes. ☐

The witch pretended to be <u>friendly</u>. ☐

The elves were <u>quite</u> peculiar. ☐

1 mark

33 Name the **word class** that the underlined words belong to.

We can go sledging <u>unless</u> it starts snowing again.

<u>If</u> it doesn't rain, we will go to the beach.

We can stay <u>until</u> the sun sets.

_____

1 mark

34 Explain how the position of the **comma** changes the meaning of the second sentence.

(i) Jan's aunt loves walking her dog and reading.

(ii) Jan's aunt loves walking, her dog and reading.

_____

_____

1 mark

35 In the following sentence, underline the **adverbial**.

The three friends agreed to meet outside the cinema.

1 mark

36 Complete the following sentence using a **relative clause**. Remember to punctuate your answer correctly.

The house, _____, was extremely old.

1 mark

37 Explain how the **conjunction** changes the meaning of the second sentence.

(i) He began to complain after he drove home.

(ii) He began to complain as he drove home.

_____

_____

1 mark

38 In the following sentence, circle the **modal verb**.

Dad told Trish that she (should) share her toys with her brother.

1 mark

39 Rewrite the following sentence in the **passive**. Remember to punctuate your answer correctly.

The headmaster congratulated the winner of the competition.

_____

1 mark

40 Insert **two commas** and a **semi-colon** in the correct places in the following passage.

In the autumn, the trees shed their leaves, making a mess everywhere. The gardeners have to work hard; they go home exhausted every evening.

1 mark

41 Circle the **three nouns** in the following sentence.

The pianist gave a brilliant performance last night.

1 mark

42 Show which sentence uses the **passive**.

Tick one.

The school team decided to enter the tournament. ☐

Every day, they practised hard. ☐

They were encouraged by their coach. ☐

Another team beat them in the final. ☐

1 mark

43 Write the **contracted form** of the underlined words in the following sentence in the box.

They <u>should have</u> tried harder!

[ ]

1 mark

44 Complete the sentence below using a word formed from the root word <u>history</u> on each line.

In her work as a _____, Melinda has to read a great many _____ documents.

1 mark

45 Write the grammatical term for the underlined words in the following sentence.

The noisy magpies have built a nest in the elm tree.

_____

1 mark

46 Circle each word that should start with a **capital letter** in the following sentence.

in   december,   mr   mantovani   is   planning   to   go   to   manchester   to   do   his   christmas   shopping.

1 mark

47 Circle the three **determiners** in the following sentence.

There   wasn't   much   fruit   left,   but   fortunately   I   found   two   pears   in   the   fruit   bowl.

1 mark

48 Insert an **apostrophe** in the correct place in the following sentence.

The childrens books were on the shelves.

1 mark

Practice Test Paper 1   17

49 Circle the three **prepositions** in the following sentence.

The library is (at) the end (of) the corridor (opposite) the stairs.   *1 mark*

50 Circle the **co-ordinating conjunction** in the following sentence.

When you leave your office, you should close the windows (and) turn off the light.   *1 mark*

END OF PRACTICE TEST PAPER 1

English Grammar, Punctuation & Spelling

Practice Test 2

KS2 SATs Year 6 — English — Paper 1: Questions

First name: _____

Middle name: _____

Last name: _____

Date of birth: _____

School name: _____

Total score: _____ / 50

1 Insert a **comma** in the correct place in the following sentence.

As Jeff was not answering his phone, I decided not to buy him a ticket. 1 mark

2 Show which sentence must end with a **question mark**.

Tick one.

How this happens on a regular basis is a mystery	☐
I wish someone would tell me how regularly this happens	☐
How regularly does this happen	☐
There is no explanation as to why this happens regularly	☐

1 mark

3 The prefix mal- can be used with the root word function to make the word **malfunction**. Tick the meaning of the word **malfunction**.

Tick one.

to fail to work	☐
to start to work	☐
to work quickly	☐
to work slowly	☐

1 mark

4 Tick **one** box in each row to show whether the sentence is a **question**, a **statement** or a **command**.

SENTENCE	Question	Statement	Command
Iguanas are insectivorous lizards			
Do you know what 'insectivorous' means			
If you don't, look it up in a dictionary			
These lizards live in many tropical regions			

1 mark

5 Add two **commas** to the following sentence to make it clear Uncle Phillip loves four things.

Our Uncle Phillip loves rowing boats fishing and rivers.

1 mark

6 Tick the **adverb** in the following sentence.

Tick one.

Trish screamed loudly as the large, hairy, deadly spider crawled towards her.

☐   ☐ ☐ ☐

1 mark

7 Insert a **pair of commas** in the correct place in the following sentence.

I've put the brown briefcase that smells a bit musty in the attic.

1 mark

8 Show which sentence is grammatically correct.

Tick one.

Last night, Iris gone to the theatre with her mother. ☐

Three weeks ago, we had no idea this would happen. ☐

In a couple of years' time, my brother will be go to university. ☐

Next Monday, it had been a bank holiday. ☐

1 mark

9 Show which word is a **synonym** of the verb <u>conflict</u>.

Tick one.

harm ☐

ignore ☐

shout ☐

clash ☐

1 mark

Practice Test Paper 2   21

10 Identify the sentence that is a **command**.

Tick one.

You need to catch the 38 bus. ☐

Take the 38 bus to Olive Road. ☐

The 38 bus will take you to Dyne Road. ☐

I must catch the 38 bus in five minutes. ☐

1 mark

11 Draw a line to match each **prefix** to a word to make **four** different words. Use each prefix only once.

Prefix	Word
de	regard
em	port
dis	body
im	value

1 mark

12 Show which option completes the sentence in the **past perfect**.

They discovered their accountant _____ all their savings.

Tick one.

has stolen ☐

is stealing ☐

was stealing ☐

had stolen ☐

1 mark

13 Show which sentence is written in **Standard English**.

Tick one.

All the cold water in the fridge had been drunk. ☐

Kelly broughted her delicious tuna salad to the picnic. ☐

Yesterday, Thomas was been gone for hours. ☐

We was planning to visit Melissa last week. ☐

1 mark

14 Identify the sentence that uses a **dash** correctly.

Tick one.

Abi enjoys drawing — mandalas their intricate designs are very satisfying. ☐

Abi enjoys drawing mandalas — their intricate designs are very satisfying. ☐

Abi enjoys — drawing mandalas their intricate designs are very satisfying. ☐

Abi enjoys drawing mandalas their intricate designs are — very satisfying. ☐

1 mark

15 Identify the grammatical term for the underlined part of the sentence.

I bumped into Robert Mason <u>the other day</u>.

Tick one.

a main clause ☐

a subordinate clause ☐

a preposition phrase ☐

an adverbial ☐

1 mark

16 Show which sentence must **not** end with an **exclamation mark**.

Tick one.

How did you get here so quickly ☐

I can't believe how quickly you arrived ☐

How remarkably fast that was ☐

No-one has ever arrived so quickly ☐

1 mark

17 Insert a **colon** in the correct place in the following sentence.

The miser loved but two things his money and the vault that kept it safe.

1 mark

18 Show which sentence uses the underlined word as a **noun**.

Tick one.

Did Rachel <u>book</u> our tickets yesterday? ☐

The average number of hours an athlete <u>trains</u> will vary. ☐

I'm sorry I can't stop; I'm in a terrible <u>hurry</u>. ☐

I prefer <u>plain</u> bagels to those with raisins. ☐

1 mark

19 Show which sentence is punctuated correctly.

Tick one.

Suddenly, the temperature dropped rapidly and, our teeth began to chatter. ☐

Suddenly the temperature dropped, rapidly and our teeth began to chatter. ☐

Suddenly the temperature, dropped rapidly and, our teeth began, to chatter. ☐

Suddenly, the temperature dropped rapidly and our teeth began to chatter. ☐

1 mark

20 Explain how the use of the **modal verb** changes the meaning of the second sentence.

(a) Chris and Omar go scuba diving in Belize.

(b) Chris and Omar could go scuba diving in Belize.

_____

_____

_____

1 mark

21 Identify the **word class** of the underlined word in the following sentence.

I haven't spoken to Jemma <u>since</u> her graduation ceremony last June.

	Tick one.
adjective	☐
preposition	☐
conjunction	☐
adverb	☐

1 mark

22 Insert a **subordinating conjunction** to show that they learnt about dolphins and were at the aquarium at the same time.

They learnt about dolphins _____ they were at the aquarium.

1 mark

23 Complete the following sentence with a **noun** formed from the verb <u>remove</u>.

The _____ of those recycling bins has been very unpopular.

1 mark

Practice Test Paper 2   25

24 Replace the underlined words with the correct **pronoun**. Write one pronoun in each box.

Whenever I stay with my aunt, <u>my aunt</u> [ ] always makes delicious food. The last time I visited, however, I insisted that <u>my aunt and I</u> [ ] do something different. I took my aunt to a restaurant so that someone else could cook for <u>my aunt</u> [ ] for a change.

1 mark

25 Show which sentence is the most **formal**.

Tick one.

Consulting the residents is probably a good move. ☐

We should consult the residents before we make our decision. ☐

The residents ought to be consulted before a decision is made. ☐

I think it would be a good idea to consult the residents first. ☐

1 mark

26 Barry wants to know where the meeting is being held. Write the **question** he could ask to find out. Remember to punctuate your sentence correctly.

_____

1 mark

27 Underline the **subject** of the following sentence.

Last Friday, a dangerous criminal escaped from a London prison.

1 mark

28 Write the name of the punctuation mark that could be used instead of commas in the following sentence.

Thankfully, within a few hours, the criminal was caught with the help of the public.

_____

1 mark

29 Circle the most **formal** option in each of the following boxes to complete the advert.

Simon & Simon, your local travel agent, is [proud / chuffed / well-pleased]

to unveil its most [gobsmacking / amazing / mind-blowing] holiday packages to date

for you and your [mates / friends / besties] this summer.

1 mark

30 Tick one box in each row to show whether the underlined noun is **singular** or **plural**.

SENTENCE	Singular	Plural
The <u>firecrackers'</u> explosions were ear-piercingly loud.		
That <u>writer's</u> horror stories are not as good as his detective novels.		
Mrs Lillian, our <u>class's</u> favourite teacher, is emigrating to Canada.		

1 mark

31 Write the **word class** of each underlined word in the spaces provided.

Rhonda always thinks <u>fast</u>. _____

Rhonda is a <u>fast</u> thinker. _____
                                                                                   1 mark

32 Show which sentence is the most **formal**.

	Tick one.
If that sugar is left out, it will attract ants.	☐
Remember to buy a loaf of sourdough bread.	☐
He is training to become a heavyweight boxer.	☐
The manager insisted Tim be fired.	☐

1 mark

33 Circle the four **prepositions** in the following sentence.

In my opinion, it would be very silly indeed to go for a walk in this torrential rain without an umbrella or a waterproof coat.

1 mark

34 Insert one **hyphen** and one **comma** in the correct places in the following sentence.

Helena's husband was an incredibly sociable good looking university lecturer.

1 mark

35 Explain how the position of the **apostrophe** changes the meaning of the second sentence.

(i) What are your student's most common mistakes?

(ii) What are your students' most common mistakes?

_____

_____

1 mark

36 Show which **two** sentences use punctuation to show **parenthesis.**

Tick two.

Despite the long queue, we waited to buy some delicious, Cornish pasties. ☐

Louis Pasteur, a French scientist, is regarded as one of the 3 founders of bacteriology. ☐

I find some fruit — particularly lychees, mangosteens and rambutans — rather odd. ☐

Unique to Mauritius, the dodo was a large, flightless bird — now long extinct. ☐

1 mark

37 Underline the **relative clause** in each of the following sentences.

The thieves needed a safe place where they could hide their loot.

A nonagon is a polygon which has nine sides.

Julia's pet hamster whose name is Squiggly always seems to be asleep.

1 mark

38 Rewrite the underlined verbs in the **simple past** tense.

Every summer holiday, the Thompson family go to the Lake District where they always

have a wonderful time.

1 mark

39 Name the grammatical term for the underlined words in the following sentence.

This is a treaty which will enable us to tackle global warming far more effectively.

1 mark

40 Tick one box in each row to show whether the sentence is written in the **active** or the **passive**.

SENTENCE	Active	Passive
The results should be announced by 5 pm.		
Troops are being sent to the border.		
The temperature has dropped since yesterday.		

1 mark

41 Rewrite the sentence below as **direct speech**. Remember to punctuate your answer correctly.

They asked if they could have some more juice.

They asked, _____

1 mark

42 Circle the **possessive pronoun** in the following sentence.

Despite the three-day-delivery promise on your website, the cake tins that I ordered from you two weeks ago still haven't arrived.

1 mark

43 Rewrite the two following sentences as one sentence using an appropriate **co-ordinating conjunction**. Remember to punctuate your answer correctly.

She was very late for her appointment. She was walking slowly.

_____

1 mark

44 Underline the **adverbial** in the following sentence.

We have been told the trial will start next Tuesday.

1 mark

45 Circle the **relative pronoun** in the following sentence.

Kyle who trains at our local gym every Thursday afternoon dislikes bananas.   1 mark

46 Add a **suffix** to the words in the boxes to complete the sentences below.

Please, be quiet: your whispering is unbelievably _____.

distract

This argument is too complex; you need to _____ it.

simple

1 mark

47 Circle each word that should begin with a **capital letter** in the following sentence.

two of my favourite nursery rhyme characters used to be old king cole and humpty dumpty.   1 mark

48 Circle the four **verbs** in the following passage.

There were several strange noises coming from the attic.

Bravely, Liam switched on his torch and headed towards the stairs.   1 mark

49 Rewrite the underlined verb in the following sentence so it is in the **present progressive**.

Unfortunately, we <u>experienced</u> difficulties with the website.

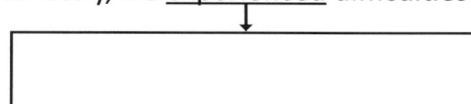

1 mark

50 Underline the **subordinate clause** in the following sentence.

We were left speechless <u>when we opened our front door</u>: there was a river of water streaming down our stairs.

1 mark

END OF PRACTICE TEST PAPER 2

English Grammar, Punctuation & Spelling

Practice Test 3

KS2 SATs Year 6 — English — Paper 1: Questions

First name: _____

Middle name: _____

Last name: _____

Date of birth: _____

School name: _____

Total score: _____ / 50

1 Draw a line to connect each word to the correct **suffix** so that it makes an **adjective**.

Word	Suffix
fiction	ive
expense	al
courage	ous

1 mark

2 Use the **conjunctions** from the box below to complete the following sentence. You may use each conjunction only **once**.

| for   as   or |

I could quite happily eat a whole pizza _____ a huge plate of pasta, _____ I'm ravenous _____ I've not eaten since yesterday.

1 mark

3 Draw a circle around the **subject** in the following sentence.

Last week, poor Mrs Mitcham had a nasty accident in the street.

1 mark

4 Draw a line to connect each sentence to the correct **determiner**. You may use each determiner only **once**.

Sentence	Determiner
____ cat killed the mouse.	an
Is there ____ explanation for this?	your
____ guess is as good as mine.	neither

1 mark

5 Identify the option that must end with a **full stop**.

Tick one.

The train won't leave yet, will it ☐

When does this train normally leave ☐

Do you know if the train has left yet ☐

When the train will leave is not yet known ☐

1 mark

6 Show which sentence uses the **colon** correctly.

Tick one.

Helen has had several pets a cat: a gerbil a hedgehog a dog and a parrot. ☐

Helen has had several pets: a cat, a gerbil, a hedgehog, a dog and a parrot. ☐

Helen has had several pets a: cat, a gerbil, a hedgehog, a dog, and a parrot. ☐

Helen has had several: pets, a cat, a gerbil, a hedgehog, a dog and a parrot. ☐

1 mark

7 Use an appropriate **adverb** to complete the following sentence.

Rihanna is _____ late for meetings.

1 mark

8 Tick two boxes to identify where the missing **inverted commas** should go in the following sentence.

☐   ☐ ☐ ☐
Are you all going swimming? Molly asked.

1 mark

Practice Test Paper 3   35

9 Put **one** comma in the correct place in the following sentence.

Quickly and quietly the thief moved around the empty house.

1 mark

10 Tick one box in each row to show whether the sentence is in the **present perfect** or the **past perfect**.

SENTENCE	Present perfect	Past perfect
Anne has been our school librarian for a year now.		
She had worked at an investment company before that.		
She has seemed a lot happier since coming to the library.		

1 mark

11 Use the correct **pronouns** to replace the underlined word in each of the following sentences.

Last week, John decided to sell <u>John's</u> old car.

Instead of buying another one, <u>John</u> bought a bicycle.

1 mark

12 Show which sentence uses the **hyphen** correctly.

Tick one.

My seven-year-old brother is very naughty. ☐

My seven year-old-brother is very naughty. ☐

My seven year-old brother is very naughty. ☐

My seven-year old brother is very naughty. ☐

1 mark

13 Identify the sentence that shows it is **least likely** to snow tomorrow.

Tick one.

It shouldn't snow tomorrow. ☐

It mightn't snow tomorrow. ☐

It won't snow tomorrow. ☐

It mayn't snow tomorrow. ☐

1 mark

14 Draw a line to connect each sentence to its correct **function**. You may use each function only once.

Sentence

| I want you to clean your grandfather's car this afternoon |
| Make sure that you remember to clean your grandfather's car today |
| When are you going to clean your grandfather's car today |
| How fantastically clean your grandfather's car looks now |

Function

| command |
| exclamation |
| statement |
| question |

1 mark

15 Identify the sentence which is written in **Non-Standard** English.

Tick one.

The wizard had forgotten where he'd left his book of spells. ☐

I went to the mall at 4 o'clock and met my friends there. ☐

Sanjay and Anita didn't do their chores yesterday. ☐

They has bought her a wonderful birthday present. ☐

1 mark

Practice Test Paper 3   37

16 (a) Identify the punctuation marks on either side of the words quite remarkably in the following sentence.

Despite the queue, we managed (quite remarkably) to buy some tickets.

_____

1 mark

(b) Name a **different** punctuation mark which could be used correctly in the same places.

_____

1 mark

17 Using the boxes given, write the **contracted forms** of the underlined words in each of the following sentences.

Their application was not accepted so they are going to reapply.

[   ]   [   ]

We have got loads of time before the flight — do not panic!

[   ]

1 mark

18 Your teacher is helping you to correct the punctuation of the sentence in the following box. Which **two** pieces of advice are you given?

| "Where is the bus station" asked? the woman |

Tick two.

There should be a question mark at the end of the sentence. ☐

There should be a full stop after the word 'station'. ☐

There should be a question mark after the word 'station', not 'asked'. ☐

There should be a comma before the word 'asked'. ☐

There should be a full stop at the end of the sentence. ☐

1 mark

19 Show which sentence uses **capital letters** correctly.

Tick one.

Last September, a group of us went to the Greek island of Crete. ☐

Last September, a group of us went to the Greek Island of Crete. ☐

Last September, a group of us went to the greek island of Crete. ☐

Last September, a group of us went to the greek Island of Crete. ☐

1 mark

20 Insert a **semi-colon** in the correct place in the following sentence.

For years, the Browns never had much money that all changed when they won the lottery.

1 mark

21 Show the meaning of the root <u>ject</u> in the word family below.

e**ject**ed   re**ject**ion   pro**ject**

Tick one.

refuse ☐

area ☐

stick ☐

throw ☐

1 mark

22 In the sentence below, circle the word that contains an **apostrophe** for **contraction**.

As they're all so muddy, Mary's boots, Jeremy's sneakers and Martin's shoes must all be taken off before the children can come into Grandma's nice clean house.

1 mark

Practice Test Paper 3   39

23 Tick one box in each row to show if the **commas** have been used correctly in the sentence.

SENTENCE	Commas used correctly	Commas used incorrectly
For this recipe, you will need, sugar, flour, eggs, and maple syrup.		
A large number of animals, including lions, tigers, wolves and hyenas, are meat-eaters.		
Jonah has visited several places in Europe: Paris, Vienna, Madrid, Athens, and, Berlin.		
The laptop, which was very old, finally stopped working.		

1 mark

24 In the sentence below, circle all the **prepositions**.

Leaning against the wall stood an old, wooden ladder under which was a rusty bucket.

1 mark

25 Rearrange the words in the following statement to turn it into a question. Use the given words only. Make sure you punctuate your answer correctly.

Statement: The children have eaten their sandwiches.

Question: _____

1 mark

26 In the sentence below, circle the two words that show the **tense**.

Now, we have a house in Manchester, but, in the past, we lived in a cottage in the countryside.

1 mark

27 In each of the following sentences, underline the **main clause**.

Linda went for a walk in the park as it was warm and sunny.

If Gill doesn't arrive in the next five minutes, we're going home.

During the summer, while he was on holiday, Val broke his arm.

1 mark

28 Circle the **conjunction** in each of the following sentences.

Tom wanted to try bungee jumping although he knew it was dangerous.

Make sure you tidy up once you've finished in the art room.

1 mark

29 In each of the following, show whether the underlined clause is a **main clause** or a **subordinate clause** by ticking one box.

SENTENCE	Main clause	Subordinate clause
The enemy spy waited patiently until the sun had gone down.		
He walked in the shadows as he did not want to be seen.		
When he was sure the hangar was empty, he crept inside.		

1 mark

30 (a) Add a **comma** to the following sentence to make it clear that **only** Hal and Raj went to the shops.

Once they'd met Ed Hal and Raj went to the shops.

1 mark

(b) Add **commas** to the following sentence to make it clear that **all** three children went to the shops.

Once they'd met Ed Hal and Raj went to the shops.

1 mark

Practice Test Paper 3   41

31 How do the different **prefixes** change the meanings of the two following sentences?

Kelly has <u>reread</u> the article.

This means that the article _____

_____

_____

Kelly has <u>misread</u> the article.

This means that the article _____

_____

_____

1 mark

32 Circle the two **prepositions** in the following sentence.

Boris, Brenda's cat, has broken the marble statuette which used to stand on the small table outside her living room.

1 mark

33 Use the correct **possessive pronoun** to replace the underlined words in each of the following sentences.

These scissors belong to <u>my uncle</u>. They are _____.

These bicycles are owned by <u>my brother and sister</u>. They are _____.

Those shoes belong to <u>my mother</u>. They are _____.

1 mark

34 (a) Explain the meaning of the word **synonym**.

_____

_____

1 mark

(b) Write one word that is a **synonym** of the word <u>rational</u>.

_____

1 mark

42   Practice Test Paper 3

35 Rewrite the verbs in the boxes below using the **present simple tense** to complete the following sentences.

This factory _____ very famous. It _____
                    ↑   ↑
                   [be]   [employ]

hundreds of workers and _____ Jaguars.
                              ↑
                        [manufacture]

1 mark

36 Using **adjectives** derived from the nouns in brackets, complete the following passage. One has been done for you.

Every year, the class choose Rosemary as their ___**favourite**___ [favour] book monitor

because she is _____ [trust]. She is also extremely _____

[care] with everyone's books.

1 mark

37 Choose the option that completes the following sentence correctly.

That child _____ mother is a famous physicist has just won a science prize.

Tick one.

who's ☐

whose ☐

whom   ☐

which ☐

1 mark

Practice Test Paper 3   43

38 Use the word <u>break</u> as a **verb** in a sentence of your own. Do not change the word. Make sure you punctuate your sentence correctly.

_____

1 mark

Use the word <u>break</u> as a **noun** in a sentence of your own. Do not change the word. Make sure you punctuate your sentence correctly.

_____

1 mark

39 In the following sentence, underline the **relative clause**.

Catherine of Aragon who was born a Spanish princess was King Henry VIII's first wife.

1 mark

40 Tick one box in each row to show if the sentence is written in the **active voice** or in the **passive voice**.

SENTENCE	Active voice	Passive voice
A gate was left open at the zoo.		
Some of the animals escaped.		
Luckily, they were all rounded up quickly.		

1 mark

41 Rewrite the following sentence so that it is written in the **passive voice**. Make sure you punctuate your sentence correctly.

A large, poisonous snake bit me.

_____

1 mark

42 Identify the two **adjectives** in the sentence below by drawing a circle around each one.

George rushed upstairs quickly to fetch his (clean) boots and a (fresh) T-shirt from his bedroom.

1 mark

43 Select the option which shows how the underlined words in the following sentence are used.

Fortunately for us, in our village, there are several excellent restaurants.

	Tick one.
as a main clause	☐
as a preposition phrase	☐
as a noun phrase	☐
as a fronted adverbial	☐

1 mark

44 Select the verb that completes the sentence in the **subjunctive form**.

It was vital that the patient _____ treated at once.

	Tick one.
were	☐
be	☐
being	☐
was	☐

1 mark

Practice Test Paper 3   45

45 Identify the function of the following sentence.

Come here at once and apologise

	Tick one.
a command	☐
an exclamation	☐
a statement	☐
a question	☐

1 mark

46 Show which sentence is written in the **past progressive form**.

	Tick one.
Brushing your teeth last thing at night is a healthy habit.	☐
At the end of the holidays, we visited Jane in Dublin.	☐
The angry cyclist was shouting at the careless driver.	☐
I had to finish reading this book before the lesson.	☐

1 mark

END OF PRACTICE TEST PAPER 3

English Grammar, Punctuation & Spelling

Practice Test 4

KS2 SATs Year 6 English — Paper 1: Questions

First name: _____

Middle name: _____

Last name: _____

Date of birth: _____

School name: _____

Total score: _____ / 50

1 Identify the sentence that must end with a **question mark**.

Tick one.

When does the train depart ☐

He didn't know when the train left ☐

I asked Bruno when the train would leave ☐

Tell me when the train departs ☐

1 mark

2 Which **pair of verbs** completes the following sentence correctly?

One hundred years ago, computers _____ unheard of; now, however, they _____ an essential part of our everyday lives.

Tick one.

was	are	☐
is	were	☐
are	were	☐
were	are	☐

1 mark

3 Draw a line to match each **prefix** to the correct word so that it makes a new word.

Prefix	Word
ir	accurate
il	national
sub	legal
inter	responsible
in	marine

1 mark

48   *Practice Test Paper 4*

4 Which sentence is punctuated correctly?

Tick one.

All around, her she could see a glistening blanket of snow. ☐

All around her she could see, a glistening blanket of snow. ☐

All around her, she could see a glistening blanket of snow. ☐

All around her she could, see a glistening blanket of snow. ☐

1 mark

5 Which of the following sentences is written in the **past tense**?

Tick one.

That beautiful painting is a self-portrait. ☐

It was completed in the nineteenth century. ☐

It is believed to be very valuable. ☐

It portrays its artist: a Frenchman. ☐

1 mark

6 Circle one word in each underlined pair to complete the sentences below using **Standard English**.

They **was / were** waiting for the bus for ages.

It **was / were** half an hour late.

1 mark

7 In the box, write the **contracted form** of the underlined words.

Ed should have arrived by now.

☐

1 mark

8 Identify the sentence that must end with an **exclamation mark**.

Tick one.

The team were badly beaten, weren't they ☐

I'll tell you why they lost ☐

Ask the manager why they didn't win ☐

What a terrible defeat for the team ☐

1 mark

9 Which sentence below uses an **apostrophe** correctly?

Tick one.

Owing to the storm, people's houses were damaged. ☐

Owing to the storm, peoples house's were damaged. ☐

Owing to the storm, peoples' houses were damaged. ☐

Owing to the storm, peoples houses' were damaged. ☐

1 mark

10 What does the word <u>few</u> refer to in the following passage?

The majority of birds in the British Isles are active during the day. However, a <u>few</u>, such as owls and nightjars, are nocturnal.

Tick one.

owls ☐

birds ☐

nightjars ☐

Isles ☐

1 mark

11 Circle **all** the **pronouns** in the following sentence.

Last week, Danny borrowed my calculator for a maths exam and, irritatingly, dropped and broke it.

1 mark

12 Complete the following sentence with an **adverb** formed from the noun conscience.

Bob is a reliable worker and can be trusted to carry out his work _____.

1 mark

13 Tick one box to show which part of the sentence is a **relative clause**.

The talented mechanic who repaired my car used to work in Germany.
☐ ☐ ☐ ☐

1 mark

14 Select the option that shows **how** the underlined words are used in the sentence.

After looking for two hours, Adam found his missing textbook under his bed.

Tick one.

as a main clause ☐

as a noun phrase ☐

as a relative clause ☐

as a preposition phrase ☐

1 mark

15 Tick one box in each row to show how **the modal verb** affects the **meaning** of each sentence.

SENTENCE	Modal verb indicates certainty	Modal verb indicates possibility
Maurice, my cousin, can speak French and Spanish.		
As odd as I know it sounds, that story could be true.		
Jim might be asleep now as he woke up at 6 am.		
I will apologise to Iris for shouting at her yesterday.		

1 mark

Practice Test Paper 4 51

16 Name the **punctuation mark** used between the two main clauses.

Unfortunately, as she is not in school today, the headmistress, Mrs Priya Singh, cannot see you: she is attending a conference in Bristol for head teachers.

_____

1 mark

17 Tick one box in each row to show whether the underlined clause is a **main clause** OR a **subordinate clause**.

SENTENCE	Main clause	Subordinate clause
<u>Even though Jennie was good at rounders</u>, she preferred tennis.		
She played at the weekends <u>whenever it was possible</u>.		
Her father, <u>who coached her</u>, had been a professional player.		

1 mark

18 Circle **all** the **conjunctions** in the following sentences.

As I had to travel to Edinburgh for work, I decided to take the overnight train on Sunday evening.

When I checked the website, I discovered many of the trains to Scotland had been cancelled.

This made me delay my journey until the trains began running normally again on Monday.

1 mark

19 Circle the two words in the following sentence that are **synonyms** of each other.

Sir Gavin was rewarded with great riches for his bravery, for, as the king told him, he admired the courage that Sir Gavin had displayed in protecting the young prince from the giant.

1 mark

20 Tick **all** the sentences that contain **a preposition**.

The soldiers fought hard, but lost the battle. ☐

We've been waiting since six o'clock. ☐

As they watched the match, it began snowing. ☐

Pip became upset after he arrived. ☐

1 mark

21 Write a sentence that uses the word promise as a **noun**. Remember to punctuate your sentence correctly.

_____

Write a sentence that uses the word promise as a **verb**. Remember to punctuate your sentence correctly.

_____

2 marks

22 In the word family below, what does the root spect mean?

inspection   spectator   spectacles

Tick one.

look ☐

test ☐

correct ☐

show ☐

1 mark

Practice Test Paper 4   53

23 Draw a line to match each word to its correct **antonym**.

Word	Antonym
liberate	genuine
responsible	undependable
insincere	hinder
assist	confine

1 mark

24 Rewrite the following sentence, adding a **subordinate clause**. Remember to punctuate your sentence correctly.

Louise and Jo swam in the sea.

_____

1 mark

25 Label the boxes below with **V (verb)**, **S (subject)** and **O (object)** to show the parts of the sentence.

<u>Sandra</u> baked a cake and <u>gave</u> <u>it</u> to her grandmother.
☐   ☐ ☐

1 mark

26 Circle all the words in the following sentences that should start with a **capital letter**.

marie is french, but she also speaks german. she has lived in berlin since april, 2012.

1 mark

27 Which sentence below is written in the **active voice**?

Tick one.

The customer has been given a free meal. ☐

The slippery road caused an accident. ☐

All the work was done by robots. ☐

Our luggage was sent to India by mistake. ☐

1 mark

28 Which sentence below is punctuated correctly?

Tick one.

The play was very good brilliant, in fact, so it was no surprise that the audience applauded loudly. ☐

The play was very good — brilliant, in fact, so it was no surprise that the audience applauded loudly. ☐

The play was very good — brilliant, in fact — so it was no surprise that the audience applauded loudly. ☐

The play was very good — brilliant, in fact, — so it was no surprise that the audience applauded loudly. ☐

1 mark

29 Tick one box to show where **a dash** should go in the following sentence.

The team knew exactly what would happen their striker would be sent off.
  ↑   ↑   ↑   ↑
  ☐   ☐   ☐   ☐

1 mark

30 Tick one box to show which sentence below uses the **present perfect**.

Tick one.

Claire has visited Greece several times. ☐

The tourists all went diving in the Aegean. ☐

After he had arrived in Athens, Sanjeev visited the Acropolis. ☐

Declan had been studying the ancient Greeks for years. ☐

1 mark

31 Which of the following sentences is a **command**?

Tick one.

We could go and have a coffee and a muffin. ☐

They had better take the rubbish out. ☐

There's a new novel you really should read. ☐

When you see Jake, tell him about the party. ☐

1 mark

32 Rewrite the following sentence as **direct speech**. Remember to punctuate your answer correctly.

Mike informed Janet that he knew where her book had been left.

Mike informed Janet, _____

_____

1 mark

33 Insert a pair of **commas** in the correct place in the following sentence.

One of the five retired racehorses which were being auctioned last weekend won the Grand National ten years ago.

1 mark

34 Tick one box in each row to show whether the underlined word is **an adjective** OR **an adverb**.

SENTENCE	Adjective	Adverb
I will see you later.		
I'm wearing my best jacket.		
The bird sang sweetly.		
The girl was lonely.		

1 mark

35 Explain how the use of the **commas** changes the meaning in these two sentences.

The children, who were in Year 6, received prizes.

The children who were in Year 6 received prizes.

_____

_____

_____

1 mark

56 *Practice Test Paper 4*

36 Which sentence below uses the **hyphen** correctly?

Tick one.

I have an up to-date version of that software. ☐

I have an up-to-date-version of that software. ☐

I have an up-to-date version of that software. ☐

I have an up-to date version of that software. ☐

1 mark

37 Rewrite the following sentence so that it is written in the **passive voice**. Remember to punctuate your answer correctly.

The angry bull chased them across the field.

_____

1 mark

38 Tick one box in each row to show if the word **until** is **a preposition** or **a subordinating conjunction**.

SENTENCE	until used as a preposition	until used as a subordinating conjunction
She can't go to school until she has completely recovered.		
You must wait here until the doctor can see you.		
He is going to be busy until the end of the month.		

1 mark

39 Complete the following table by adding a **suffix** to each noun to make an **adjective**.

Noun	Adjective
truth	
coward	
debate	
feather	
man	

1 mark

40 Tick one box in each row to show whether the underlined conjunction is a **subordinating conjunction** or a **co-ordinating conjunction**.

SENTENCE	Subordinating conjunction	Co-ordinating conjunction
Polly remained calm <u>although</u> I let out a blood-curdling scream.		
<u>When</u> I was finally able to speak, Polly asked me what was wrong.		
When I looked at her, I saw that she was smiling, <u>so</u> I stopped feeling guilty.		

1 mark

41 Complete the following sentence so that it uses the **subjunctive form**.

Is it necessary that she _____ there?

1 mark

42 Circle **all** the **determiners** in the following sentence.

Ten   soldiers   marched   back   to   their   camp   early   this   morning.

1 mark

43 Underline the longest possible **noun phrase** in the following sentence.

The   cunning   thief   denied   that   he   had   stolen   all   of   Lady   Herbert's   valuable

paintings   and   jewels.

1 mark

44 Underline the **verb form** that is in the **present perfect** in the following passage.

Pompeii, in Southern Italy, was buried in ash when Mount Vesuvius erupted

in A.D. 79. Today, it has become an important tourist attraction that is visited

by thousands of people who want to see how the ancient Romans lived.

1 mark

45 Write a sentence that lists all the information given in the following box. Remember to punctuate your answer correctly.

> **To make a kite**
>
> a heavy-duty plastic bag
>
> electrical tape
>
> a line
>
> a plastic winder
>
> 2 rods

_____

_____

_____

_____

_____

1 mark

46 Complete the following sentence with a **possessive pronoun**.

Sally is a friend of _____.

1 mark

47 Circle the **adverb** in the following sentence.

Delia often meets her friends at the local sports centre after school.

1 mark

48 Insert a **colon** in the correct place in the following sentence.

That author's books are always exciting: each one she has written is full of thrilling adventures.

1 mark

49 Which **punctuation mark** should be used in the place indicated by the arrow?

When we decided to have a barbecue, we invited Mr Brown and his son, John Paul was asked to come as well.

Tick one.

question mark ☐

ellipsis ☐

comma ☐

full stop ☐

1 mark

END OF PRACTICE TEST PAPER 4

Practice Test Papers 1, 2, 3 & 4

ANSWERS & MARKING GUIDELINES

Notes to Using the Answers & Marking Guidelines

Before using the Answers, please note the following:

MARKS
- After the correct answer to each question is given, the marking guidelines indicate **how many marks** each answer is worth.
- Half marks **may not be awarded** under any circumstances.

MULTIPLE ANSWERS
- When a question requires **more than one answer, ALL** the student's given **responses must be correct** for their answer to be regarded as right. For example, if the correct answers to a question are the words *his* and *him*, the student must provide both correct words.
- When a question can be **correctly answered in more than one way**, this is noted in this section and an **example** of at least **one possible correct** answer is given.

ADDITIONAL MARKING GUIDANCE
- Where necessary, additional marking guidance has been supplied in italics, including, on occasion, student responses **which cannot be accepted**.

ANSWERS TO 'TICK BOX' QUESTIONS
- Where the student has to show their chosen answer by ticking at least one box, this section gives the correct answer(s), followed by which box(es) should be ticked: *1st box, 2nd box, 3rd box, etc.*
  - For sets of vertical boxes, the topmost box is the 1st box, and so on.
  - For sets of horizontal boxes, the leftmost box is the 1st box, and so on.

PRACTICE TEST PAPER 1: ANSWERS & MARKING GUIDELINES

(1) How did you do that **(2ND BOX)**
Award 1 MARK for the correct answer.

(2) power → less; child → hood; comfort → able; amuse → ment
Award 1 MARK for ALL 4 correct answers.

(3) Don't scare... → command;
Don't forget... → command;
Don't you ever... → question;
Don't go near... → command
Award 1 MARK for ALL 4 correct answers.

(4) Katy was late for school **again,** so she began to run.
Award 1 MARK for the correctly placed COMMA.

(5) dis → appoint; mis → take; sub → marine; in → secure
Award 1 MARK for ALL 4 correct answers.

(6) Make sure you take an umbrella **(4TH BOX)**
Award 1 MARK for the correct answer.

(7) I; were; likes
Award 1 MARK for ALL 3 correct answers.

(8) *Answers will differ, but MUST all be CORRECTLY SPELT & WRITTEN IN LOWER CASE. Examples:*
- The film <u>which</u> I watched yesterday was...
- The film <u>that</u> I watched yesterday was...

Award 1 MARK for an appropriate RELATIVE PRONOUN that has been correctly inserted.

(9) The mayor is going to <u>present</u> the prizes. **(4TH BOX)**
Award 1 MARK for the correct answer.

(10) Jane wanted to play **tennis;** her brother preferred to have a game of squash.
Award 1 MARK for the correctly placed SEMI-COLON.

(11) The orang-utan **(**one of the great apes**)** is an endangered species.
Award 1 MARK for the correctly placed PAIR OF BRACKETS.

(12) between **(2ND BOX)**
Award 1 MARK for the correct answer.

(13) Some tourists — probably from Germany — asked me the way to the station. **(2ND BOX)**
Award 1 MARK for the correct answer.

(14) abandoned **(3RD BOX)**
Award 1 MARK for the correct answer.

(15) Would you care for another cup of tea? **(1ST BOX)**
Award 1 MARK for the correct answer.

(16) 4TH BOX
The correct place for the missing hyphen is as follows:
Bernie had some carrot sticks, cherry tomatoes, a banana and a **sugar-free** drink for lunch.
Award 1 MARK for the correct answer.

(17) a preposition **(3RD BOX)**
Award 1 MARK for the correct answer.

(18) courageous; valiant
Award 1 MARK for BOTH correct answers.

(19) main clause
Award 1 MARK for a correct answer.
ALSO ACCEPT answers that use an abbreviation that makes the intention clear. Example:
- main

DO NOT ASSESS punctuation or spelling here.

(20) Nobody could find Jason — he was hiding in the garden.
Award 1 MARK for the correctly placed DASH.

(21) a co-ordinating conjunction **(1ST BOX)**
Award 1 MARK for the correct answer.

(22) Aunt May refuses to go **camping:** she is afraid of being bitten or stung by insects or creepy crawlies.
Award 1 MARK for the correctly placed COLON.

(23) Gerald enjoys **swimming,** playing **basketball,** rock **climbing,** reading detective novels and making models.
Award 1 MARK for ALL 3 correctly placed COMMAS.

(24) When Patrick said he had finished his homework, his mother looked surprised. **(4TH BOX)**
Award 1 MARK for the correct answer.

(25) I will call you on our return.
Award 1 MARK for the correct answer.

(26) remain
Award 1 MARK for the correct answer.

(27) <u>We</u> → S (subject); <u>cake</u> → O (object); <u>Giles</u> → S (subject); <u>it</u> → O (object)
Award 1 MARK for ALL 4 correct answers.

(28) ...Susie <u>goes</u> to... → went;
...always <u>swims</u> ten... → swam
Award 1 MARK for BOTH correct answers.
DO NOT ACCEPT any misspellings of the verb forms.

(29) Danny's leg is broken now. **(1ST BOX)**
Award 1 MARK for the correct answer.

(30) exhausted; steep; unwell
Award 1 MARK for ALL 3 correct answers.

(31) Harry asked hopefully, "Is there anything for supper?" **(2ND BOX)**
Award 1 MARK for the correct answer.

(32) The elves were <u>quite</u> peculiar. **(4TH BOX)**
Award 1 MARK for the correct answer.

(33) conjunction OR conjunctions OR subordinating conjunctions
Award 1 MARK for a correct answer.
DO NOT ASSESS punctuation or spelling here.

(34) *Answers will differ and may refer to either or both of the sentences. Examples:*
- In the first sentence, Jan's aunt loves two things.
- The second sentence means that Jan's aunt loves three things.
- In sentence (i) the two things Jan's aunt loves are walking her dog and reading, but in sentence (ii) the three things Jan's aunt loves are walking, her dog and reading.

Award 1 MARK for an answer that shows a correct understanding that THERE ARE 3 NAMED ACTIVITIES IN THE 2ND SENTENCE.
DO NOT ACCEPT general answers. Example:
- It's a list.

DO NOT ASSESS punctuation or spelling here.

(35) outside the cinema
Award 1 MARK for the correct answer.

(36) *Answers will differ, but MUST all be a GRAMMATICALLY CORRECT RELATIVE CLAUSE. Examples:*
- The house, <u>which was deserted</u>, was extremely old.
- The house, <u>that stood on the corner</u>, was extremely old.

Award 1 MARK for a correct answer.
DO NOT ACCEPT answers which are grammatically incorrect. Example:
- The house, <u>what was owned by Mr Smith</u>, was extremely old.

(37) *Answers will differ and may refer to either or both of the sentences. Examples:*
- In the first sentence, he drove home first, then he began to complain.
- The second sentence means he began to complain at the same time he was driving home.
- In sentence (i) it tells us what he did after he drove home, but in sentence (ii) it tells us what he did when he was driving home.

Award 1 MARK for an answer that shows a correct understanding that THE CONJUNCTION CHANGES THE CHRONOLOGICAL RELATIONSHIP BETWEEN THE ACTIONS.
DO NOT ACCEPT general answers. Example:
- It changes when he did it.

DO NOT ASSESS punctuation or spelling here.

(38) should
Award 1 MARK for the correct answer.

(39) *Answers will differ, but MUST all be CORRECTLY PUNCTUATED SENTENCES that CORRECTLY USE THE PASSIVE VOICE. Examples:*
- The winner of the competition was congratulated.
- The winner of the competition was congratulated by the headmaster.

Award 1 MARK for a correct answer.
DO NOT ACCEPT misspellings of the verb forms or answers which change the verb or the tense.

(40) In the **autumn,** the trees...their **leaves,** making...work **hard;** they go...
Award 1 MARK for BOTH the correctly placed COMMAS and SEMI-COLON.

(41) pianist; performance; night
Award 1 MARK for ALL 3 correct answers.

(42) They were encouraged by their coach. **(3RD BOX)**
Award 1 MARK for the correct answer.

(43) should have → should've
Award 1 MARK for the correct answer.
DO NOT ACCEPT misspellings.

(44) historian; historical
Award 1 MARK for BOTH correct answers.
DO NOT ACCEPT misspellings or words written in upper case.

(45) noun phrase(s)
Award 1 MARK for a correct answer.
ALSO ACCEPT expanded / extended noun phrase OR grammatical function (i.e. subject).
DO NOT ASSESS punctuation or spelling here.

(46) in december, mr mantovani is planning to go to **manchester** to do his **christmas** shopping.
Award 1 MARK for ALL 6 correct answers.

(47) much; two; the
Award 1 MARK for ALL 3 correct answers.

(48) The **children's** books were on the shelves.
Award 1 MARK for the correctly placed APOSTROPHE.

(49) at; of; opposite
Award 1 MARK for ALL 3 correct answers.

(50) and
Award 1 MARK for the correct answer.

PRACTICE TEST PAPER 2: ANSWERS & MARKING GUIDELINES

(1) As Jeff was not answering his **phone,** I decided not to buy him a ticket.
Award 1 MARK for the correctly inserted COMMA.

(2) How regularly does this happen (**3RD BOX**)
Award 1 MARK for the correct answer.

(3) to fail to work (**1ST BOX**)
Award 1 MARK for the correct answer.

(4) Iguanas are insectivorous... → statement;
Do you know... → question;
If you don't... → command;
These lizards live... → statement
Award 1 MARK for ALL 4 correct answers.

(5) Our Uncle Phillip loves **rowing, boats,** fishing and rivers.
Award 1 MARK for BOTH correctly inserted COMMAS.

(6) loudly (**1ST BOX**)
Award 1 MARK for the correct answer.

(7) I've put the brown **briefcase,** that smells a bit **musty,** in the attic.
Award 1 MARK for the correctly inserted PAIR OF COMMAS.

(8) Three weeks ago, we had no idea this would happen. (**2ND BOX**)
Award 1 MARK for the correct answer.

(9) clash (**4TH BOX**)
Award 1 MARK for the correct answer.

(10) Take the 38 bus to Olive Road. (**2ND BOX**)
Award 1 MARK for the correct answer.

(11) de → value; em → body; dis → regard; im → port
Award 1 MARK for ALL 4 correct answers.

(12) had stolen (**4TH BOX**)
Award 1 MARK for the correct answer.

(13) All the cold water in the fridge had been drunk. (**1ST BOX**)
Award 1 MARK for the correct answer.

(14) Abi enjoys drawing mandalas — their intricate designs are very satisfying. (**2ND BOX**)
Award 1 MARK for the correct answer.

(15) an adverbial (**4TH BOX**)
Award 1 MARK for the correct answer.

(16) How did you get here so quickly (**1ST BOX**)
Award 1 MARK for the correct answer.

(17) The miser loved but two **things:** his money and the vault that kept it safe.
Award 1 MARK for the correctly placed COLON.

(18) I'm sorry I can't stop; I'm in a terrible <u>hurry</u>. (**3RD BOX**)
Award 1 MARK for the correct answer.

(19) Suddenly, the temperature dropped rapidly and our teeth began to chatter. (**4TH BOX**)
Award 1 MARK for the correct answer.

(20) *Answers will differ and may refer to either or both of the sentences. Examples:*
- *In the first sentence, they definitely go scuba diving in Belize.*
- *In the second sentence, it means perhaps they will go scuba diving in Belize.*
- *In sentence (a) Chris and Omar certainly go scuba diving in Belize, but in sentence (b) they may go scuba diving in Belize.*

Award 1 MARK for an answer that CORRECTLY shows that the modal verb 'COULD' INDICATES UNCERTAINTY OR POSSIBILITY. DO NOT ASSESS punctuation or spelling here.

(21) preposition (**2ND BOX**)
Award 1 MARK for the correct answer.

(22) *Answers will differ, but MUST all be CORRECTLY SPELT. Example:*
- *They learnt about dolphins <u>when</u> they were at the aquarium.*

Award 1 MARK for an appropriate SUBORDINATING CONJUNCTION that has been correctly inserted.

(23) removal OR removing
Award 1 MARK for a correct answer.
DO NOT ACCEPT any misspellings.

(24) ...aunt, <u>my aunt</u> always... → she;
...that <u>my aunt and I</u> do... → we;
...cook for <u>my aunt</u> for a... → her
Award 1 MARK for ALL 3 correctly spelt PRONOUNS.

(25) The residents ought to be consulted before a decision is made. (**3RD BOX**)
Award 1 MARK for the correct answer.

(26) *Answers will differ, but MUST all use CORRECT QUESTION PUNCTUATION. Examples:*
- *Where is the meeting being held?*
- *"Where is the meeting being held?"*

Award 1 MARK for a correct answer.
DO NOT ACCEPT answers in which the question is contained in a sentence. Example: Barry asked, "Where is the meeting being held?"

(27) a dangerous criminal OR criminal
Award 1 MARK for a correct answer.

(28) dash OR dashes OR (a) pair of dashes OR brackets OR (a) pair of brackets
Award 1 MARK for a correct answer.
DO NOT ASSESS punctuation or spelling here.

(29) proud; amazing; friends
Award 1 MARK for ALL 3 correctly identified WORDS.

(30) The <u>firecrackers'</u> explosions... → plural;
That <u>writer's</u> horror... → singular;
...our <u>class's</u> favourite... → singular
Award 1 MARK for ALL 3 correct answers.

(31) ...thinks <u>fast</u> → adverb;
...<u>fast</u> thinker → adjective
Award 1 MARK for BOTH correct answers.
DO NOT ASSESS punctuation or spelling here.

(32) The manager insisted Tim be fired. **(4TH BOX)**
Award 1 MARK for the correct answer.

(33) In; for; in; without
Award 1 MARK for ALL 4 correct answers.

(34) Helena's husband was an incredibly **sociable, good-looking** university lecturer.
Award 1 MARK for BOTH the correctly placed COMMA and HYPHEN.

(35) Answers will differ and may refer to either or both of the sentences. Examples:
- In the first sentence, there is only one student.
- The second sentence means there is more than one student.
- In the second sentence, it shows plural possession.
- In sentence (i) there is one student, but in sentence (ii) there is more than one student.

Award 1 MARK for an answer that shows a correct understanding of the PLURAL POSSESSIVE APOSTROPHE.
DO NOT ASSESS punctuation or spelling here.

(36) Louis Pasteur, a French scientist, is regarded as one of the 3 founders of bacteriology. **(2ND BOX)**
I find some fruit — particularly lychees, mangosteens and rambutans — rather odd. **(3RD BOX)**
Award 1 MARK for BOTH correct answers.

(37) where they could hide their loot;
which has nine sides;
whose name is Squiggly
Award 1 MARK for ALL 3 correct answers.

(38) ...family <u>go</u> to... → went;
...always <u>have</u> a... → had
Award 1 MARK for BOTH correct answers.
DO NOT ACCEPT any misspellings of the verb forms.

(39) (a) relative clause OR (a) subordinate clause
Award 1 MARK for a correct answer.
DO NOT ASSESS punctuation or spelling here.

(40) The results should... → passive;
Troops are being... → passive;
The temperature has... → active
Award 1 MARK for ALL 3 correct answers.

(41) *Answers will differ, but MUST all be an APPROPRIATE, GRAMMATICALLY CORRECT and CORRECTLY PUNCTUATED sentence in DIRECT SPEECH. Example:*
- They asked, "Can we have some more juice?"

Award 1 MARK for a correct answer.

(42) your
Award 1 MARK for the correct answer.

(43) *Answers will differ, but MUST all be a GRAMMATICALLY CORRECT and CORRECTLY PUNCTUATED sentence that uses an APPROPRIATE CO-ORDINATING CONJUNCTION. Example:*
- She was very late for her appointment, <u>yet</u> she was walking slowly.

Award 1 MARK for a correct answer.

(44) next Tuesday
Award 1 MARK for the correct answer.

(45) who
Award 1 MARK for the correct answer.

(46) distract → distracting;
simple → simplify
Award 1 MARK for BOTH correct answers.
DO NOT ACCEPT any misspellings.

(47) **two** of my favourite nursery rhyme characters used to be **old king cole** and **humpty dumpty**.
Award 1 MARK for ALL 6 correct answers.

(48) were; coming; switched; headed
Award 1 MARK for ALL 4 correct answers.

(49) <u>experienced</u> → are experiencing
Award 1 MARK for the correct answer.
DO NOT ACCEPT any misspellings of the verb forms.

(50) when we opened our front door
Award 1 MARK for the correct answer.

PRACTICE TEST PAPER 3: ANSWERS & MARKING GUIDELINES

(1) fiction → al; expense → ive; courage → ous
Award 1 MARK for ALL 3 correct answers.

(2) I could quite happily eat a whole pizza **or** a huge plate of pasta, **for** I'm ravenous **as** I've not eaten since yesterday.
Award 1 MARK for ALL 3 correctly inserted CONJUNCTIONS.

(3) Mrs Mitcham OR poor Mrs Mitcham
Award 1 MARK for a correct answer.

(4) ____ cat killed the mouse. → neither;
Is there ____ explanation for this? → an;
____ guess is as good as mine. → your
Award 1 MARK for ALL 3 correct answers.

(5) When the train will leave is not yet known **(4TH BOX)**
Award 1 MARK for the correct answer.

(6) Helen has had several pets: a cat, a gerbil, a hedgehog, a dog and a parrot. **(2ND BOX)**
Award 1 MARK for the correct answer.

(7) *Answers will differ, but MUST all be CORRECTLY SPELT. Example:*
- Rihanna is <u>never</u> late for meetings.

Award 1 MARK for the correct insertion of an appropriate ADVERB.

(8) 1ST BOX & 2ND BOX
The correct places for the missing inverted commas are as follows: "Are you all going swimming?" Molly asked.
Award 1 MARK for BOTH correct answers.

(9) Quickly and **quietly,** the thief moved around the empty house.
Award 1 MARK for the correctly inserted COMMA.

(10) Anne has been... → present perfect;
She had worked... → past perfect;
She has seemed... → present perfect
Award 1 MARK for ALL 3 correct answers.

(11) ...sell <u>John's</u> old... → his;
...one, <u>John</u> bought... → he
Award 1 MARK for BOTH correct PRONOUNS.

(12) My seven-year-old brother is very naughty. **(1ST BOX)**
Award 1 MARK for the correct answer.

(13) It won't snow tomorrow. **(3RD BOX)**
Award 1 MARK for the correct answer.

(14) I want you... → statement;
Make sure that... → command;
When are you... → question;
How fantastically clean... → exclamation
Award 1 MARK for ALL 4 correct answers.

(15) They has bought her a wonderful birthday present. **(4TH BOX)**
Award 1 MARK for the correct answer.

(16a) brackets OR a pair of brackets
Award 1 MARK for a correct answer.

(16b) commas OR a pair of commas OR dashes OR a pair of dashes
Award 1 MARK for a correct answer.

(17) ...application <u>was not</u> accepted... → wasn't;
...so <u>they are</u> going... → they're;
<u>We have</u> got... → We've
Award 1 MARK for ALL 3 correct answers.
DO NOT ACCEPT the use of the pronoun 'We' without a capital letter in this instance (i.e. we've).

(18) There should be a question mark after the word 'station', not 'asked'. **(3RD BOX)**
There should be a full stop at the end of the sentence. **(5TH BOX)**
Award 1 MARK for BOTH correct answers.

(19) Last September, a group of us went to the Greek island of Crete. **(1ST BOX)**
Award 1 MARK for the correct answer.

(20) For years, the Browns never had much **money;** that all changed when they won the lottery.
Award 1 MARK for the correctly placed SEMI-COLON.

(21) throw **(4TH BOX)**
Award 1 MARK for the correct answer.

(22) they're
Award 1 MARK for the correct answer.

(23) For this recipe... → commas used incorrectly;
A large number... → commas used correctly;
Jonah has visited... → commas used incorrectly;
The laptop, which... → commas used correctly
Award 1 MARK for ALL 4 correct answers.

(24) against; under
Award 1 MARK for BOTH correct answers.

(25) Have the children eaten their sandwiches?
Award 1 MARK for the correct answer.

(26) have; lived
Award 1 MARK for BOTH correct answers.

(27) Linda went for a walk in the park;
we're going home;
Val broke his arm
Award 1 MARK for ALL 3 correct answers.

(28) although; once
Award 1 MARK for BOTH correct answers.

(29) The enemy spy waited patiently... → main clause;
...as he did not want to be seen → subordinate clause;
...he crept inside → main clause
Award 1 MARK for ALL 3 correct answers.

(30a) Once they'd met **Ed,** Hal and Raj went to the shops.
Award 1 MARK for the correctly placed COMMA.

(30b) Once they'd **met, Ed,** Hal and Raj went to the shops.
Award 1 MARK for BOTH correctly placed COMMAS.
DO NOT ACCEPT the use of a serial comma: Once they'd met, Ed, Hal, and Raj went to the shops.

(31) *Answers will differ, but must CORRECTLY explain the MEANINGS of the verbs 'REREAD' and 'MISREAD'. Examples:*
- Kelly has reread the article. → This means that the article has been read again.
- Kelly has misread the article. → This means that the article has not been understood correctly.

Award 1 MARK for BOTH correct EXPLANATIONS.

(32) on; outside
Award 1 MARK for BOTH correct answers.

(33) ...to my uncle → his;
...by my brother and sister → theirs;
...to my mother → hers
Award 1 MARK for ALL 3 correct answers.

(34a) *Answers will differ. Example:*
- Synonyms are words that mean the same thing.

Award 1 MARK for a correct DEFINITION.

(34b) *Answers will differ. Example:*
- logical.

Award 1 MARK for a correct SYNONYM.

(35) be → is; employ → employs; manufacture → manufactures
Award 1 MARK for ALL 3 correct answers.
DO NOT ACCEPT misspellings of any of the verb forms.

(36) trust → trustworthy; care → careful
Award 1 MARK for BOTH correct ADJECTIVES.
ALSO ACCEPT trust → trusted.
DO NOT ACCEPT misspellings of the adjectives.

(37) whose **(2ND BOX)**
Award 1 MARK for the correct answer.

(38) *Answers will differ for each part of this question.*
Award 1 MARK for a GRAMMATICALLY CORRECT and CORRECTLY PUNCTUATED sentence that uses 'BREAK' as a VERB. Example:
- I didn't mean to break your watch.

DO NOT ACCEPT answers that change the given form of the verb. Example: I'm sorry I broke your watch.

Award 1 MARK for a GRAMMATICALLY CORRECT and CORRECTLY PUNCTUATED sentence that uses 'BREAK' as a NOUN. Example:
- The children played hopscotch during break.

DO NOT ACCEPT answers that change the given form of the noun. Example: Luke takes far too many breaks at work.

(39) who was born a Spanish princess
Award 1 MARK for the FULL correct answer.

(40) A gate was... → passive voice;
Some of the animals... → active voice;
Luckily, they were... → passive voice
Award 1 MARK for ALL 3 correct answers.

(41) I was bitten by a large, poisonous snake.
Award 1 MARK for a CORRECTLY PUNCTUATED sentence in the PASSIVE VOICE.
ALSO ACCEPT I was bitten.

(42) clean; fresh
Award 1 MARK for BOTH correct answers.

(43) as a fronted adverbial **(4TH BOX)**
Award 1 MARK for the correct answer.

(44) be **(2ND BOX)**
Award 1 MARK for the correct answer.

(45) a command **(1ST BOX)**
Award 1 MARK for the correct answer.

(46) The angry cyclist was shouting at the careless driver. **(3RD BOX)**
Award 1 MARK for the correct answer.

PRACTICE TEST PAPER 4: ANSWERS & MARKING GUIDELINES

(1) When does the train depart (**1ST BOX**)
Award 1 MARK for the correct answer.

(2) were are (**4TH BOX**)
Award 1 MARK for the correct answer.

(3) ir → responsible; il → legal; sub → marine; inter → national; in → accurate
Award 1 MARK for ALL 5 correct answers.

(4) All around her, she could see a glistening blanket of snow. (**3RD BOX**)
Award 1 MARK for the correct answer.

(5) It was completed in the nineteenth century. (**2ND BOX**)
Award 1 MARK for the correct answer.

(6) They <u>were</u> waiting for the bus for ages.
It <u>was</u> half an hour late.
Award 1 MARK for BOTH correct answers.

(7) Ed <u>should have</u> arrived... → should've
Award 1 MARK for the correct answer.

(8) What a terrible defeat for the team (**4TH BOX**)
Award 1 MARK for the correct answer.

(9) Owing to the storm, people's houses were damaged. (**1ST BOX**)
Award 1 MARK for the correct answer.

(10) birds (**2ND BOX**)
Award 1 MARK for the correct answer.

(11) my; it
Award 1 MARK for BOTH correctly identified PRONOUNS.

(12) conscientiously
Award 1 MARK for the correct ADVERB formed from CONSCIENCE.
DO NOT ACCEPT misspellings.

(13) who repaired my car (**2ND BOX**)
Award 1 MARK for the correct answer.

(14) as a noun phrase (**2ND BOX**)
Award 1 MARK for the correct answer.

(15) Maurice, my cousin, can speak... → certainty;
...that story could be... → possibility;
Jim might be asleep... → possibility;
I will apologise to Iris... → certainty
Award 1 MARK for ALL 4 correct answers.

(16) colon

Award 1 MARK for the correct answer.
ALSO ACCEPT plausible misspellings.

(17) <u>Even though Jennie was good at rounders</u> → subordinate clause;
<u>whenever it was possible</u> → subordinate clause;
<u>who coached her</u> → subordinate clause
Award 1 MARK for ALL 3 correct answers.

(18) **As** I had...;
When I checked...;
...my journey **until** the trains...
Award 1 MARK for ALL 3 correctly identified CONJUNCTIONS.

(19) bravery = courage
Award 1 MARK for BOTH correctly identified SYNONYMS.

(20) We've been waiting since six o'clock. (**2ND BOX**)
Award 1 MARK for THE ONE correctly identified sentence.

(21) *Answers will differ for each part of this question.*
Award 1 MARK for a GRAMMATICALLY CORRECT and CORRECTLY PUNCTUATED sentence that uses 'PROMISE' as a NOUN.
Example:
- I made her a solemn <u>promise</u>.

DO NOT ACCEPT answers that change the given form of the noun. Example: Alex always keeps his <u>promises</u>.

Award 1 MARK for a GRAMMATICALLY CORRECT and CORRECTLY PUNCTUATED sentence that uses 'PROMISE' as a VERB.
Example:
- I <u>promise</u> to be good.

DO NOT ACCEPT answers that change the given form of the verb. Example: I <u>have promised</u> to be good.

(22) look (**1ST BOX**)
Award 1 MARK for the correct answer.

(23) liberate ≠ confine; responsible ≠ undependable; insincere ≠ genuine; assist ≠ hinder
Award 1 MARK for ALL 4 correct answers.

(24) *Answers will differ, but MUST all be GRAMMATICALLY CORRECT, CONTAIN A SUBORDINATE CLAUSE and be CORRECTLY PUNCTUATED. Example:*
- Louise and Jo<u>, who are best friends,</u> swam in the sea.

Award 1 MARK for a correct answer.
DO NOT ACCEPT punctuation mistakes; the use of a phrase instead of a subordinate clause; or the addition of another main clause.

(25) <u>Sandra</u> → S (subject); <u>gave</u> → V (verb); <u>it</u> → O (object)
Award 1 MARK for ALL 3 correct answers.

(26) **marie** is **french**, but she also speaks **german. she** has

lived in **berlin** since **april**, 2012.
Award 1 MARK for ALL 6 correct answers.

(27) The slippery road caused an accident. **(2ND BOX)**
Award 1 MARK for the correct answer.

(28) The play was very good — brilliant, in fact — so it was no surprise that the audience applauded loudly. **(3RD BOX)**
Award 1 MARK for the correct answer.

(29) 3RD BOX
The correct place for the dash is as follows: The team knew exactly what would happen — their striker would be sent off.
Award 1 MARK for the correct answer.

(30) Claire has visited Greece several times. **(1ST BOX)**
Award 1 MARK for the correct answer.

(31) When you see Jake, tell him about the party. **(4TH BOX)**
Award 1 MARK for the correct answer.

(32) Mike informed Janet, "I know where your book has been left."
Award 1 MARK for the correct answer.

(33) One of the five retired **racehorses,** which were being auctioned last **weekend,** won the Grand National ten years ago.
Award 1 MARK for BOTH correctly placed COMMAS.

(34) ...see you later → adverb;
...my best jacket → adjective;
...bird sang sweetly → adverb;
...girl was lonely → adjective
Award 1 MARK for ALL 4 correct answers.

(35) *Answers will differ, but MUST all FULLY EXPLAIN BOTH SENTENCES. Example:*
- The first sentence means that the children who received prizes happened to be in Year 6. The second sentence means that ALL the children who were in Year 6 received prizes.

Award 1 MARK for A FULL EXPLANATION OF BOTH SENTENCES.
ALSO ACCEPT answers that are not written in full sentences.
DO NOT ACCEPT answers that explain only one sentence or which explain the use of the comma in general.

(36) I have an up-to-date version of that software. **(3RD BOX)**
Award 1 MARK for the correct answer.

(37) *Answers will differ, but MUST all be CORRECTLY PUNCTUATED SENTENCES that CORRECTLY USE THE PASSIVE VOICE. Examples:*
- They were chased.
- They were chased across the field by the angry bull.

Award 1 MARK for a correct answer.
DO NOT ACCEPT answers which change the verb or the tense.

(38) ...school until she has... → subordinating conjunction;
...here until the doctor... → subordinating conjunction;
...busy until the end... → preposition
Award 1 MARK for ALL 3 correct answers.

(39) *Answers will differ for some nouns, but they MUST all be CORRECTLY SPELT. Examples:*
- truth → truthful OR truthless
- coward → cowardly
- debate → debated OR debatable
- feather → feathery OR featherless OR feather-like
- man → manly OR manlike OR mannish.

Award 1 MARK for 5 correct answers.
ALSO ACCEPT answers using capital letters.

(40) although → subordinating conjunction;
When → subordinating conjunction;
so → co-ordinating conjunction
Award 1 MARK for ALL 3 correct answers.

(41) *Answers will differ. Example:*
- Is it necessary that she go there?

Award 1 MARK for a correct answer.
DO NOT ACCEPT answers using capital letters.

(42) Ten; their; this
Award 1 MARK for ALL 3 correct answers.

(43) all of Lady Herbert's valuable paintings and jewels
Award 1 MARK for the correct FULL NOUN PHRASE.

(44) has become
Award 1 MARK for the correct answer.

(45) *Answers will differ, but MUST all be CORRECTLY PUNCTUATED. Example:*
- You need the following things to make a kite: a heavy-duty plastic bag, electrical tape, a line, a plastic winder and 2 rods.

Award 1 MARK for a correctly punctuated LIST.
ALSO ACCEPT answers which correctly separate the items using semi-colons; contain misspellings; and that change the order of the items in the list.
DO NOT ACCEPT answers omitting any item or listing the items using bullet points.

(46) *Answers will differ. Example:*
- Sally is a friend of mine.

Award 1 MARK for a correct answer.
DO NOT ACCEPT answers that use a possessive determiner and a noun, e.g. my sister's.

(47) often
Award 1 MARK for the correct answer.

(48) That author's books are always **exciting:** each one she has written is full of thrilling adventures.
Award 1 MARK for the correctly placed COLON.

(49) full stop **(4TH BOX)**
Award 1 MARK for the correct answer.

Printed in Great Britain
by Amazon